MAR 1 4 2016

YŎGI BEAR'S™

GUIDE TO ANIMAL TRACKS

by Mark Weakland   illustrated by Christian Cornia

Consultant:
Dr. John D. Krenz
Department of Biology
Minnesota State University
Mankato, Minnesota

CAPSTONE PRESS
a capstone imprint

It was fall in Jellystone Park. An early snow covered the ground in a thin blanket of white. Walking through the woods, Yogi Bear and Boo Boo came upon some tracks.

"Hey, hey, hey," said Yogi. "Someone else is out walking today."

"I wonder who left those tracks," said Boo Boo.

"Good question, little buddy," said Yogi. "Let's study them and find the answer."

"Really?" asked Boo Boo.

Yogi smiled. "Come on, Boo Boo. A track is a clue."

"What do you mean, Yogi?" asked Boo Boo.

"Tracks give information," said Yogi. "For example, we cannot see the animals, but we know they are around. How? We see their tracks. Different animals leave different tracks. Tracks tell us how many and what species of animals live in the forest."

tracks made
by one animal

tracks made by two
different animals

tracks made by an
animal moving quickly

"Tracks come in patterns," said Yogi. "Patterns help us identify what animal left the track."

Boo Boo pointed to some tracks. "A pattern!"

"That is a hopping pattern," said Yogi. "What animal hops?"

rabbit
track

9

Boo Boo thought. "A rabbit hops," he said. "A squirrel hops too."

"And who is hiding under yonder bush?" asked Yogi. "Why, a bunny rabbit."

"Are there other patterns besides hopping?" asked Boo Boo.

"Of course," said Yogi. "One is a walking pattern. Another is a bounding pattern."

walking pattern
from a fox

hopping pattern
from a squirrel

bounding pattern
from a weasel

"Tracks can also be organized by shape," said Yogi. "For example, some tracks show toe marks."

"These look like two big tear drops," said Boo Boo.

Yogi grinned. "A track with two large oval marks is made by an animal with hooves, like a deer or a moose."

moose track

"Small tracks showing four toes and claw marks come from animals like foxes," said Yogi. "Tracks from a bobcat or cougar have four toes but no claw marks."

"What about big tracks with four toes and claw marks?" asked Boo Boo.

14

"That's a wolf," said Yogi.

"How do you know the tracks are from a wolf?" asked Boo Boo.

"Wolves usually walk in a straight line," said Yogi.

fox track

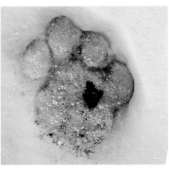

cougar track

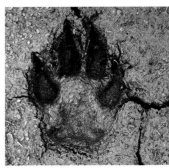

wolf track

"More tracks!" cried Boo Boo.

"Our track-makers have company," said Yogi. "I wonder who is brave enough to be out on such a cold day."

"Let's follow the tracks and find out," said Boo Boo excitedly.

"Look, Yogi," said Boo Boo. "Tracks in the mud."

"Tracks in the mud are even easier to see than tracks in the snow," said Yogi. "Look for animal tracks in wet places, like mudflats, rain puddles, and riverbanks."

"Or on the beach," said Boo Boo. "Some animals leave tracks in wet sand."

dog track in sand

dog track in snow

"These tracks are tiny," said Boo Boo. "And the toes are long!"

"Other animals make tracks with long toe marks," said Yogi. "Tiny tracks with long toes probably were made by mouse paws. Or the tracks could be from a chipmunk."

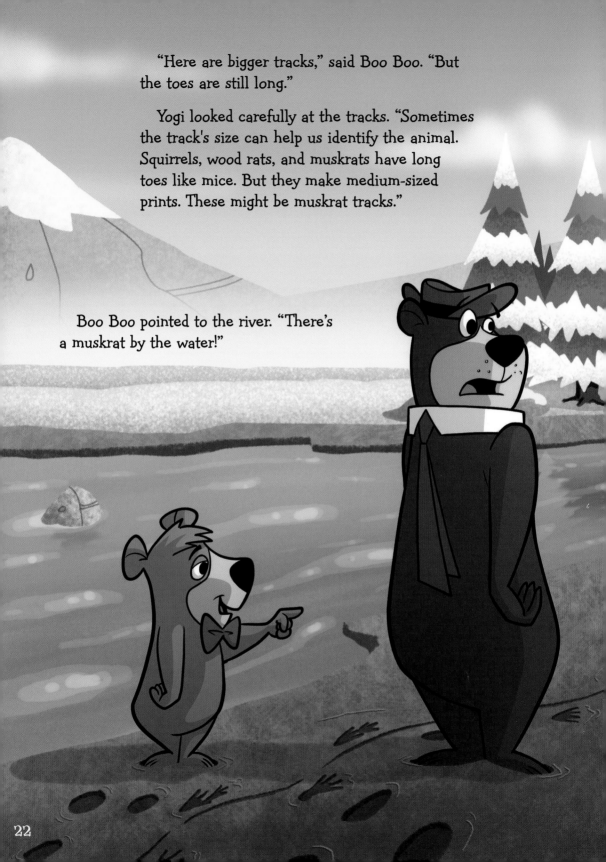

"Here are bigger tracks," said Boo Boo. "But the toes are still long."

Yogi looked carefully at the tracks. "Sometimes the track's size can help us identify the animal. Squirrels, wood rats, and muskrats have long toes like mice. But they make medium-sized prints. These might be muskrat tracks."

Boo Boo pointed to the river. "There's a muskrat by the water!"

pigeon tracks

turkey tracks

Pigeon tracks look similar to wild turkey tracks.
But they are much smaller.

"Wow," said Boo Boo. "These tracks look like human hand prints. But they are *so* small. Were they made by a baby?"

Yogi smiled. "That would be one cold baby! Opossums and raccoons leave prints that look a little like human hands. And who do we see walking by the river?"

"Raccoons!" exclaimed Boo Boo.

raccoon track

"Another set of tracks, Yogi," said Boo Boo.

"Prints from boots," observed Yogi. "A human left those."

The bears followed the tracks over the hill.
At the bottom they found Ranger Smith, standing
in the snow. He was looking at two sets of prints.

"Well, well, well," said Ranger Smith. "If it isn't Yogi and Boo Boo. You two sure know how to get around."

"Hello, Ranger Smith," said Boo Boo. "Do you know who made those tracks?"

"Of course," said Ranger Smith. "Those are bear tracks. You two have been walking in circles!"

EXPLORE MORE!

Finding animal tracks outdoors can be fun. To find animal tracks in your area, you have to look carefully and be patient. Animal tracks can be found in forests, fields, beaches, and on dirt roads. You can even find tracks in a city on a snowy day.

What You Need

- ✦ an adult
- ✦ a notebook or a piece of paper
- ✦ a pencil

What You Do

- ✦ Ask an adult to take you to different places that may have animal tracks.
- ✦ When you find animal tracks, write down where you found them and the date.
- ✦ Study the tracks and write down what you see. What do they look like? What kind of animal do you think made the tracks?
- ✦ Visit the same place one week later. Did you find animal tracks again? Are they the same kinds of tracks, or are they different?
- ✦ Visit the same place one month later. What new tracks do you see?

Places to Find Animal Tracks

- ✦ Find a place where there is mud or wet sand. Look in the woods or in fields for places wet from rain or floodwater.
- ✦ Dirt roads that have mud puddles after a heavy rain are good places to see animal tracks.
- ✦ Wet sand is also a good place to find tracks. If you live near an ocean, ask an adult to help you look on the beach.
- ✦ Go outside when it starts to snow. Even if you live in a city, you can find tracks on the sidewalk and in the parks on a snowy day.

Check out common animal tracks at **www.capstoneKids.com**.

Critical Thinking Using the Common Core

1. Animal tracks can give us information about the animal that made them. Name two things we can learn from animal tracks. (Key Ideas and Details)

2. Rabbit tracks make a hopping pattern. What is a pattern? (Craft and Structure)

3. Look at the three tracks on page 15. How are they different? How are they similar? (Integration of Knowledge and Ideas)

GLOSSARY

bobcat—a small wild cat with reddish-brown fur, black spots, and a short tail

bound—to move forward quickly with leaps and jumps

clue—something that helps you find an answer to a question or a mystery

cougar—a large wild cat with a small head, long legs, and strong body

hoof—the hard covering on an animal's foot; moose, deer, and horses have hooves

identify—to tell what something is

mudflat—an area of muddy land covered by water

muskrat—a small animal with webbed back feet, a flat tail, and thick, brown fur

opossum—a gray, furry animal that lives mostly in trees and carries its young in a pouch

pattern—a repeating set of colors, shapes, or numbers

raccoon—an animal with rings on its tail and black and white face markings that look like a mask

riverbank—the high ground on each side of a river

species—a group of plants or animals that share similar features; members of the same species can mate and have offspring

READ MORE

Buller, Laura. *Tracking.* Boys' Life Series. New York: DK Publishing. 2013.

Llewellyn, Claire. *Forests.* Habitat Survival. Chicago: Raintree. 2013.

Posada, Mia. *Who Was Here?: Discovering Wild Animal Tracks.* Minneapolis: Millbrook Press. 2014.

INTERNET SITES

FactHound offers a safe, fun way to find Internet sites related to this book. All of the sites on FactHound have been researched by our staff.

Here's all you do:

Visit *www.facthound.com*

Type in this code: 9781491465455

Super-cool stuff! Check out projects, games and lots more at **www.capstonekids.com**

INDEX

Published by Capstone Press.
1710 Roe Crest Drive, North Mankato, Minnesota 56003
www.capstonepub.com

Library of Congress Cataloging-in-Publication Data
Weakland, Mark, author.
Yogi Bear's guide to animal tracks / by Mark Weakland.
pages cm. — (Warner Brothers. Yogi Bear's guide to the great outdoors)
Summary: "Popular cartoon character Yogi Bear introduces young readers to different animal tracks, and what tracks can tell us about the animals that made them" — Provided by publisher.
Audience: Ages 6–7
Audience: K to grade 3
Includes bibliographical references and index.
ISBN 978-1-4914-6545-5 (library binding)
ISBN 978-1-4914-6549-3 (eBook PDF)
1. Animal tracks—Identification—Juvenile literature. 2. Yogi Bear (Fictitious character)—Juvenile literature. I. Warner Bros. II. Title. III. Title: Guide to animal tracks.
QL768.W37 2015
591.47'9—dc23   2014048921

Editorial Credits
Michelle Hasselius, editor; Ashlee Suker, designer;
Nathan Gassman, creative director; Tracy Cummins,
media researcher; Laura Manthe, production specialist

Image Credits
Shutterstock: Andrey Yushkov, 11 Middle, Bob Keefer, 15 Middle, Bob Orsillo, 23 Left, Gertjan Hooijer, 11 Top, JeyArt, 7 Top, Keith Tarrier, 15 Left, mycteria, 7 Bottom, 19 Right, Pi-Lens, 15 Right, PooPix, 19 Left, Richard Schramm, 9, Sharon Day, 23 Right, 25, Zoltan Major, 7 Middle, JRLPhotographer, 12, saga1966, 11 Bottom.

Printed in the United States of America in
North Mankato, Minnesota.   042015   008823CGF15

Books in this Series:

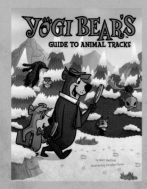